BUTTERFLY

by Jessica Rudolph

Consultant: Dr. Robin Elizabeth Thomson
Curator, Insect Collection
Department of Entomology, University of Minnesota
St. Paul, Minnesota

BEARPORT
PUBLISHING

New York, New York

Credits

Cover, © StevenRussellSmithPhotos/Shutterstock; Title Page, © Butterfly Hunter/Shutterstock; TOC, © Mariola S/Shutterstock; 4–5, © Lisa Thornberg/iStock; 5, © Le Do/Shutterstock; 6, © Perry Correll/Shutterstock; 7, © PeterJSeager/iStock; 7B, © Peter Waters/Shutterstock; 8–9, © Cathy Keifer/Shutterstock; 10, © Dennis Walker/Socal Butterflies; 11, © AttaBoyLuther/iStock; 12, © Cathy Keifer/Shutterstock; 13, © Dawna Moore/Alamy; 14, © Cameramannz/Shutterstock; 15, © Amanda Melones/Dreamstime; 16, © StevenRussellSmithPhotos/Shutterstock and © All For You/Shutterstock; 17T, © StevenRussellSmithPhotos/Shutterstock and © All For You/Shutterstock; 17B, © Peter Waters/Shutterstock; 18, © Laurie Barr/Shutterstock; 19, © Goran Kapor/Shutterstock; 20, © Kim Howell/Shutterstock and © Cathy Keifer/Shutterstock; 21, © DebraLee Wiseberg/iStock; 22, © 8ran/iStock; 23 (T to B), © StevenRussellSmithPhotos/Shutterstock, © Mathisa/Shutterstock, © Martin Mecnarowski/Shutterstock, © Pong Wira/Shutterstock, and © tea maeklong/Shutterstock; 24, © jps/Shutterstock.

Publisher: Kenn Goin
Editor: J. Clark
Creative Director: Spencer Brinker
Design: Debrah Kaiser
Photo Researcher: Thomas Persano

Library of Congress Cataloging-in-Publication Data

Names: Rudolph, Jessica.
Title: Butterfly / by Jessica Rudolph.
Description: New York, New York : Bearport Publishing, 2017. | Series: See them grow | Includes bibliographical references and index. | Audience: Ages 5 to 8.
Identifiers: LCCN 2016038814 (print) | LCCN 2016045495 (ebook) | ISBN 9781684020386 (library) | ISBN 9781684020904 (ebook)
Subjects: LCSH: Butterflies—Development—Juvenile literature.
Classification: LCC QL544.2 .R83 2017 (print) | LCC QL544.2 (ebook) | DDC 595.78/9—dc23
LC record available at https://lccn.loc.gov/2016038814

For more information, write to Bearport Publishing Company, Inc., 45 West 21st Street, Suite 3B, New York, New York 10010. Printed in the United States of America.

10 9 8 7 6 5 4 3 2

Contents

Butterfly

A monarch butterfly flutters toward a flower.

It has a small black body and big orange wings.

Butterflies are **insects**.

How did it get that way?

A butterfly starts life inside a tiny egg.

An egg forms when male and female butterflies **mate**.

After mating, the female lays an egg on a milkweed plant.

The egg is only about the size of the head of a pin.

enlarged egg

Male butterflies have two black dots on their wings. Females don't have these dots.

black dots

About four days after the egg is laid, a tiny caterpillar chews a hole in the egg.

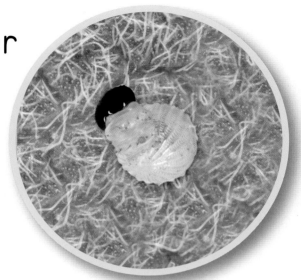

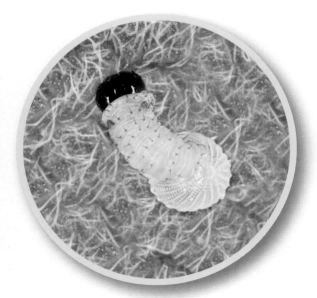

The newborn wriggles free.

It has a black head.

It has a white body and several pairs of legs.

The caterpillar's first meal is the egg case.

Crunch, crunch, crunch.

The newly hatched animal spends most of its time eating.

It eats milkweed leaves.

The caterpillar gets bigger and bigger.

It forms black, white, and yellow stripes.

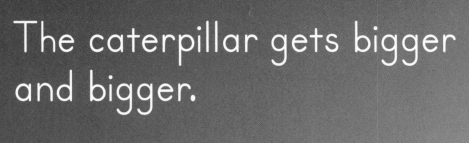

A caterpillar has strong jaws to chomp on leaves.

In order to grow, the caterpillar sheds its old skin.

This is called **molting**.

Over two weeks, the little insect will molt four times.

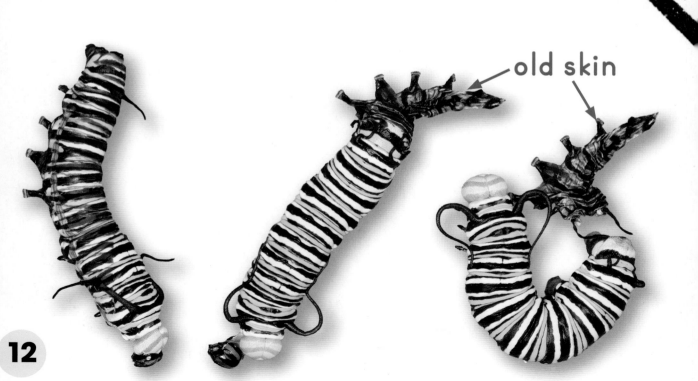

old skin

When it's not molting, the caterpillar continues to eat and eat!

13

When it's about 2 inches (5 cm) long, the caterpillar stops growing.

Then it finds a stem or branch and spins a pad of silk.

It hangs upside down from the pad.

A **chrysalis** starts to form around the caterpillar's body.

The caterpillar uses a body part called a spinneret to make silk.

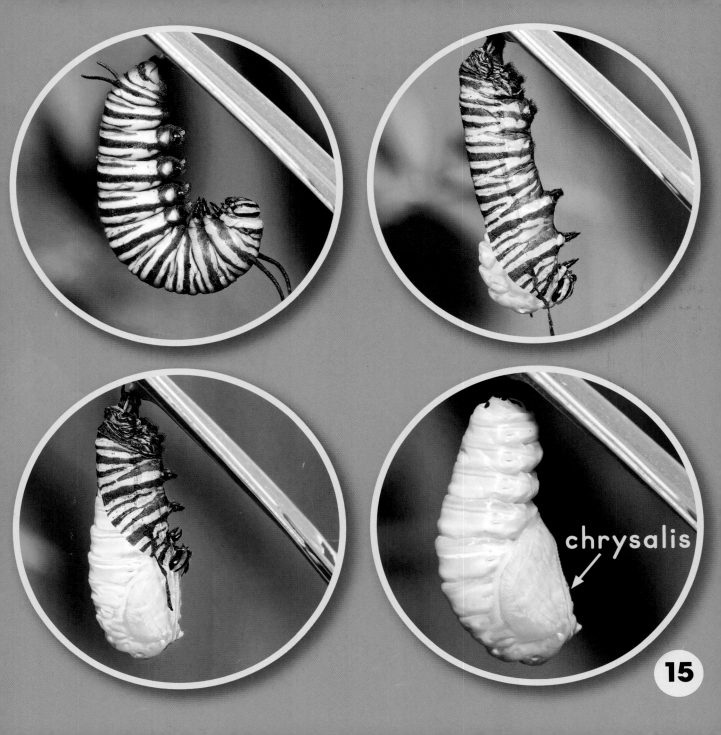

chrysalis

The chrysalis starts off green with gold flecks.

Inside, the caterpillar's body goes through lots of changes.

Soon, orange, black, and white colors can be seen.

These are the wings of the butterfly.

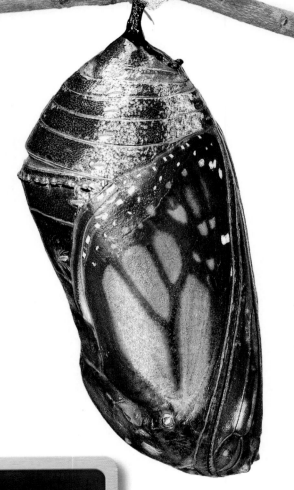

A butterfly's wings are covered in powdery **scales**.

After ten days, the chrysalis starts to shake.

Suddenly, it splits open.

A butterfly breaks free!

empty
chrysalis

At first, the
butterfly's wings are
damp and crumpled.

The butterfly moves its wings back and forth.

The wings fan out.

In the sunlight, they become dry.

Soon, the beautiful butterfly takes off!

Some monarch butterflies live for only two weeks. Others live for up to nine months.

Butterfly Facts

❀ A female monarch butterfly may lay about 700 eggs in a few weeks.

❀ Butterflies drink liquid called nectar from flowers. They use a straw-like body part called a proboscis (pruh-BOSE-uhss) to suck up the nectar.

❀ Some monarch butterflies travel north in the summer months and south in the winter months. One monarch may fly thousands of miles!

Glossary

 **chrysalis** (KRISS-uh-liss) a hard shell that protects a caterpillar as it changes into a butterfly

 **insects** (IN-sekts) small animals with six legs, three main body parts, two antennae, and a hard covering called an exoskeleton

 **mate** (MAYT) to come together to have young

 **molting** (MOHLT-ing) shedding a covering called an exoskeleton so that a new one can form

 **scales** (SKAYLZ) small overlapping sections that cover the bodies of some animals

Index

Read More

Lawrence, Ellen. *A Butterfly's Life (Animal Diaries: Life Cycles).* New York: Bearport (2012).

Markovics, Joyce. *Monarch Butterflies (In Winter, Where Do They Go?).* New York: Bearport (2015).

Learn More Online

To learn more about butterflies, visit
www.bearportpublishing.com/SeeThemGrow

About the Author

Jessica Rudolph lives in Connecticut. She has edited and written many books about history, science, and nature for children.